All my Love

Compiled by Anna Trimiew

Harold Shaw Publishers
Wheaton, Illinois

The compiler gratefully acknowledges Leland and Elsa Stewart for permission to reprint portions of Elsa's letter to Leland on their sixteenth anniversary.

Designed by David LaPlaca

ISBN 0-87788-506-0

[Library of Congress Cataloging in Publication Data applied for]

02 01 00 99 98 97
10 9 8 7 6 5 4 3 2 1

All About Love

The Joy of Romance

The Art of Loving

Preferring Each Other

An Enduring Relationship

The Joy of Romance

Falling in Love

She's got most of the symptoms—is twittery and cross, doesn't eat, lies awake, and mopes in corners.

Louisa May Alcott, Little Women

Love is the fairest flower that blooms in God's garden.

Anonymous

"How was it?" my mother asked the next morning. . . . and then I remembered and began to understand how it was. It was wonderful, that's how it was. It was absolutely wonderful.

Annie Dillard, An American Childhood

There is nothing holier, in this life of ours, than the first consciousness of love—the first fluttering of its silken wings.

Henry Wadsworth Longfellow

Love stretches your heart and makes you big inside.

Margaret Walker, Jubilee

Allow your relationship to begin at its own pace, think peacefully about it, and row it "gently down the stream." Remember, you are in the boat together, and you will be rewarded with four merrilys for every three times you row gently.

Hugh and Gayle Prather, I Will Never Leave You

Love is the queen of the graces; it outshines all the others, as the sun the lesser planets.

Thomas Watson

Kindness is the insignia of a loving heart.

Anonymous

Very often what comes first is simply a delighted preoccupation with the Beloved—a general, unspecified preoccupation with her in her totality.

C. S. Lewis, The Four Loves

We rejoice and delight in you;
we will praise your love more than wine.
How right they are to adore you!

Song of Songs 1:4

He wanted to kiss her long before he did, but when they
finally got around to it, it seemed natural and sweet and
promising.

Camilla R. Bittle, Friends of the Family

Falling in love is like springtime. We feel as though we will
be happy forever. We cannot imagine not loving our partner.
It is a time of innocence. Love seems eternal. It is a magical
time when everything seems perfect and works effortlessly.
Our partner seems to be the perfect fit. We effortlessly
dance together in harmony and rejoice in our good fortune.

John Gray, Ph.D., Men Are from Mars, Women Are from Venus

There is no surprise more wonderful than the surprise of
being loved.

Charles Morgan

[When we fall in love] we have fulfilled the law (toward one person) by loving our neighbor as ourselves. It is an image, a foretaste, of what we must become to all if Love Himself rules in us without a rival.

C. S. Lewis, The Four Loves

I compare you, my love,
to a mare among Pharaoh's chariots.
Your cheeks are comely with ornaments,
your neck with strings of jewels.
We will make you ornaments of gold,
studded with silver.

Song of Songs 1:9-11, NRSV

Love will open your mind like the chaste leaf in the morning when the sun first touches it.

Woie Soyinka, The Lion and the Jewel

Love looks not with the eyes, but with the mind,
And therefore is wingèd Cupid painted blind.

William Shakespeare, A Midsummer Night's Dream

At the touch of love everyone becomes a poet.

Plato

I thought Godfrey Cambridge was one of the prettiest men I had ever seen. His features had the immutability of a Benin mask, and his white teeth were like flags of truce. His skin was the color of rich black dirt along the Arkansas River. He was tall and big and spoke English with the staccato accent of a New York-born descendant of West Indian parents. He was definitely the one.

Maya Angelou, The Heart of a Woman

Ah, you are beautiful, my love;
ah, you are beautiful;
your eyes are doves.
Ah, you are beautiful, my beloved,
truly lovely.

Song of Solomon 1:15-16, NRSV

The Sunday evening service had just begun when a late-arriving man in a wheelchair rolled by and parked in the

aisle two pews ahead of me. As he faced the pulpit, I noticed he looked very distinguished, and his features were tanned with California sun. I couldn't help wondering, Where is his girlfriend—or wife? Maybe he was single, but even if he was, how could I ever hope to meet him?

Ginny Carr, Waiting Hearts

Falling in love is a delicious experience, obsessing, delightful, fatiguing, exhilarating, frustrating, wonderful, terrifying.

Andrew M. Greeley, Faithful Attraction

Ian and Cicely had been going together since ninth grade. They were planning to get married after college, although sometimes Cicely teased him and said she'd have to see who else asked her, first. "Change the name and not the letter, change for worse and not for better," she said. But then she would move over and into Ian's lap and wrap her arms around his neck. She smelled of baby powder, warm and pink.

Anne Tyler, Saint Maybe

Love's Springtime

I thank God for the people in this here world that tries to spread love to all kind of people. Cause, chile, can you imagine what this world would be like without em?

J. California Cooper, Family

A relationship is like a garden. If it is to thrive it must be watered regularly.

John Gray, Ph.D., Men Are from Mars, Women Are from Venus

So the Lord God caused the man to fall into a deep sleep; and while he was sleeping, he took one of the man's ribs and closed up the place with flesh. Then the Lord God made a woman from the rib he had taken out of the man, and he brought her to the man.

The man said,

"This is now bone of my bones
    and flesh of my flesh;

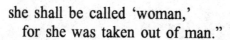

she shall be called 'woman,'
   for she was taken out of man."

For this reason a man will leave his father and mother and be united to his wife, and they will become one flesh.

Genesis 2:21-24

God created a very good twofold humanity: male and female, open to each other as equal partners. Between them sprang up openness, mutuality, reciprocity, and interdependence, as God intended.

James H. Olthuis, I Pledge You My Troth

You can give without loving, but you cannot love without giving.

Amy Carmichael

It is quite clear that between love and understanding there is a very close link. It is so close that we never know where the one ends and the other begins.

Paul Tournier, To Understand Each Other

If the commitment between a man and a woman is given insufficient importance in their lives, it will wither like a plant without water. The whole world knows that much. But fewer lovers seem to realize that extreme dependency can be just as deadly.

Dr. James C. Dobson, Love Must Be Tough

He loves but little who tells how much he loves.

John Boys

I assume that love is a power, and that it enables us before it obligates us.

Lewis B. Smedes, Love Within Limits

Arise, my love, my fair one,
and come away;
for now the winter is past,
the rain is over and gone.
The flowers appear on the earth;
the time of singing has come,
and the voice of the turtledove

is heard in our land.
The fig tree puts forth its figs,
and the vines are in blossom;
they give forth fragrance.
Arise, my love, my fair one,
and come away.

Song of Solomon 2:10-13, NRSV

The pleasure of love is in loving. We are happier in the passion we feel than in what we inspire.

François La Rochefoucauld, Reflections

In real love you want the other person's good. In romantic love you want the other person.

Margaret Anderson, The Fiery Fountain

Brevity may be the soul of wit, but not when someone's saying, "I love you." And even though he insists it would take forever to count the ways in which he loves you, let him start counting.

Judith Viorst, Love and Guilt and the Meaning of Life, etc.

Love is like a baby, it needs to be treated gently.

Anonymous, Congo

You have stolen my heart, my
sister, my bride;
you have stolen my heart
with one glance of your eyes,
with one jewel of your necklace.
How delightful is your love,
my sister, my bride!
How much more pleasing is
your love than wine,
and the fragrance of your
perfume than any spice!

Song of Songs 4:9-10

Remember how our love began?
Years ago, I offered you my arm
that September night when we first went out.
you reached for it
as we leaped a puddle together.

19

Then you walked just close enough
to show you liked it.
I glimpsed your face under the streetlight,
excitement splashing gently on it. . . .
No commitment—just beginnings.

Harold Myra, Love Notes to Jeanette

Oh, love is warm when it is new,
And love is sweet when it is true. . . .

"The Water Is Wide," American folk song

I would this maid knows more of love than I. Then when
love's first touch comes, it will not burn, but rather, glow.

Robyn Carr, The Troubadour's Romance

The heart is a mystery—not a puzzle that can't be solved,
but a mystery in the religious sense: unfathomable, beyond
manipulation, showing traces of the finger of God at work.

Thomas Moore, Soul Mates

Splendid Devotion

Whatever our souls are made of, his and mine are the same.

Emily Brontë, Wuthering Heights

Bonding refers to the emotional covenant that links a man and woman together for life and makes them intensely valuable to one another. It is the specialness that sets those two lovers apart from every person on the face of the earth. It is God's gift of companionship to those who have experienced it.

Dr. James C. Dobson, Love Must Be Tough

We love because he first loved us.

1 John 4:19

To love deeply in one direction makes us more loving in all others.

Anne-Sophie Swetchine, The Writings of Madame Swetchine

21

Sometimes love flows easily and automatically; at other times it requires effort. Sometimes our hearts are full and at other times we are empty.

John Gray, Ph.D., Men Are from Mars, Women Are from Venus

Carry each other's burdens, and in this way you will fulfill the law of Christ.

Galatians 6:2

Comfort—warm, easy, natural, accepting—is the day-to-day glue that allows a couple to have an enjoyable and peaceful coexistence.

Michael S. Broder, Ph.D., The Art of Staying Together

Let your love be like the misty rains, coming softly, but flooding the river.

Anonymous, Madagascar

Love is, above all, the gift of oneself.

Jean Anouilh, Ardèle

Love is the power that moves us to seek others.

Lewis B. Smedes, Love Within Limits

Personal meaning and human value arise only in relation-ship. Solitude casts doubt on them. Identity, too, is discovered only in relationship. Lacking companions at the level of the soul, I finally cannot find my soul. It always takes another person to show myself to me.

Walter Wangerin, Jr., As for Me and My House

There must be no "if" clauses in our relationship with others, no conditions attached to becoming involved with them. There is one love which breaks down all barriers—the love of Jesus Christ.

H. Norman Wright, Quiet Times for Couples

I would like to have engraved inside every wedding band, Be kind to one another. This is the Golden Rule of mar-riage, and the secret of making love last through the years.

Randolph Ray, My Little Church around the Corner

How beautiful you are and
how pleasing,
O love, with your delights! . . .
I belong to my lover,
and his desire is for me.

Song of Solomon 7:6, 10

The taste of good relationship is sweet, and it is enjoyed in
regions of our being that nothing else can enter.

Dr. Larry Crabb, Men & Women

One does not fall into love; one grows into love, and love
grows in him.

Karl Menninger

When one is in love, a cliff becomes a meadow.

Anonymous, Ethiopia

"The secret of a great marriage is to show your spouse
every day—and even verbalize it, if necessary—how much

you love her and how glad you are that you get to spend your whole life with her."

Husband, quoted in *The Triumphant Marriage,* by Neil Clark Warren, Ph.D.

Familiar acts are beautiful through love.

Percy Bysshe Shelley

Love is when it's 10 P.M., and you get this gnawing need for fudge-brownie ice cream, and even though you're not sick or pregnant, he drives to Baskin-Robbins and buys you some. Note: If he goes around telling people about it at parties, deduct twenty points from his score.

Judith Viorst, Love and Guilt and the Meaning of Life, etc.

Love abides. It never fails . . . it abides throughout this life and into the next in its simple form—the power that moves us toward another without expecting a reward.

Lewis B. Smedes, Love Within Limits

The Art of Loving

Faithful Attraction

We all begin with a growing sense of elation and expansion, a sense of promise that seems bigger than life. And sooner or later we all stumble.

Barry Dym, Ph.D., and Michael L. Glenn, M.D., Couples

After the fantasy side of the initial attraction begins to fade, it may give way to something that is more real, more lasting, and more grounded in everyday life than that semi-hazy state of being in love.

Michael S. Broder, Ph.D., The Art of Staying Together

Many athletes in training soon discover that their commitment requires more discipline than they bargained for. Isn't marriage the same?

H. Norman Wright, Quiet Times for Couples

Faith, though it hath sometimes a trembling hand, it must

not have a withered hand, but must stretch.

Thomas Watson

My life is a very, very happy one. It's a happiness of being connected, of knowing that there is someone I can trust completely, and that the one I trust is the one I love. I also know that the one she loves is definitely the one she can trust.

Bill Cosby

Place me like a seal over your heart,
like a seal on your arm;
for love is as strong as death. . . .
Many waters cannot quench love;
rivers cannot wash it away.

Song of Songs 8:6-7

She lifted the braided cord and for a moment cradled the small pouch of fragrant dried flowers in her hand. It brought back so many memories of the prince. "He loves me," she thought. "I'll not give him up easily. . . ."

Roberta Kells Dorr, Solomon's Song

Love doesn't grow on trees like apples in Eden—it's something you have to make. And you must use your imagination to make it too, just like anything else. It's all work, work.

Joyce Cary

There are no marriage manuals. It's just as well. If there were, no one would get married. It would be like reading a book on how babies are born. They both sound worse than they are.

Erma Bombeck, A Marriage Made in Heaven . . . or Too Tired for an Affair

While tough-minded marriage counselors and educators and church persons normally dismiss romantic love, my impression is that it is only the periodic renewal of romantic love which sustains many marriages.

Andrew M. Greeley, Faithful Attraction

We want a relationship in which we can test our half-baked ideas without shame or pretense and give voice to our deepest fears. We want a partner who sees us as unique and irreplaceable.

Judith Wallerstein and Sandra Blakeslee, The Good Marriage

Love does not begin and end the way we seem to think it does. Love is a battle, love is a war; love is growing up.

James Baldwin

Now Laban had two daughters; the name of the older was Leah, and the name of the younger was Rachel. . . . Rachel was lovely in form, and beautiful. Jacob was in love with Rachel and said, "I'll work for you seven years in return for your younger daughter Rachel."

Laban said, "It's better that I give her to you than to some other man. Stay here with me." So Jacob served seven years to get Rachel, but they seemed like only a few days to him because of his love for her.

Genesis 29:16-20

Perhaps, after all, romance did not come into one's life with pomp and blare, like a gay knight riding down; perhaps it crept to one's side like an old friend through quiet ways; perhaps it revealed itself in seeming prose, until some sudden shaft of illumination flung athwart its pages betrayed the rhythm and the music; perhaps . . . perhaps . . . love unfolded naturally out of a beautiful friendship, as a golden-hearted rose slipping from its green sheath.

Lucy Maud Montgomery, Anne of Avonlea

Those individuals who constantly hover over their partners, drawing their complete reason for existence from that one person, actually handicap the relationship. They interfere with the natural "breathing" that proves to be so healthy over the years.

Dr. James C. Dobson, Love Must Be Tough

I find it true, more each time it happens,
that I cannot be right with God
when I'm not right with you.

Harold Myra, Love Notes to Jeanette

The power of selfless love works only within the tissue of our self-interested lives.

Lewis B. Smedes, Love Within Limits

A long-term marriage has to move beyond chemistry to com-

patibility, to friendship, to companionship. It is certainly not that passion disappears, but that it is conjoined with other ways of love.

Madeleine L'Engle, Two-Part Invention

I've decided to stick with love.

Martin Luther King, Jr.

Love dies only when growth stops.

Pearl S. Buck

You and your spouse are artists bringing to the canvas of each other's life the potential that God has placed there. Your statements and beliefs about your partner will help to shape that person.

H. Norman Wright, Quiet Times for Couples

Love's Summer

Enjoy life with your wife, whom you love, all the days of this . . . life that God has given you under the sun.

Ecclesiastes 9:9

Throughout the summer of our love we realize our partner is not as perfect as we thought, and we have to work on our relationship. Not only is our partner from another planet, but he or she is also a human who makes mistakes and is flawed in certain ways.

John Gray, Ph.D., Men Are from Mars, Women Are from Venus

Above all, maintain constant love for one another, for love covers a multitude of sins.

1 Peter 4:8, NRSV

Charity offereth honey to a bee without wings.

John Trapp

Love sustains and supports all things. Everything rests on the power of love.

Lewis B. Smedes, Love Within Limits

It is a very pleasant morning, and I think of you all the time and love you with the happiest tears in my eyes.

Elizabeth Prentiss, writing to her absent husband, in More Love to Thee: The Life and Letters of Elizabeth Prentiss, *by George Lewis Prentiss*

Most of us treasure the assurance and security of living with the one we love. But at times we all miss the edge of courtship. All the advice about "dating your mate" misses the point: Courtship is surprise. There's magic in the unknown; it's the stuff of fantasy. Unless your spouse goes on your date night in disguise, even the most intimate restaurant-booth-for-two setting won't recapture the early feelings.

We *know* what our wife or husband thinks of us. We know what they look like when they're home sick with stomach flu. There's a certain security in that. But we all have a basic need for surprise, for discovery. The richest marriages I know are those where the partners say, "She keeps surprising me, keeps growing. After fifteen years I'm still finding out things about this woman." Or, "He continues to reveal unsuspected depths. He's much bigger than the man I married."

Elizabeth Cody Newenhuyse, Strong Marriages, Secret Questions

Our human tendency is to measure love by its eloquence— the beauty of its expression, how romantic or how elevated it makes us feel. But this is not the essence of love.

Eugenia Price, Make Love Your Aim

The richest love is that which submits to the arbitration of time.

Lawrence Durrell, Clea

Consistency—that's what gives a marriage relationship stability and security. Consistency means being steady. You can count on it today and tomorrow. Consistency includes determination, patience, and strength.

H. Norman Wright, Quiet Times for Couples

Frustration and disappointment arise; weeds need to be uprooted and plants need extra watering under the hot sun.

It is no longer easy to give love and get the love we need. We discover that we are not always happy, and we do not always feel loving. It is not our picture of love.

John Gray, Ph.D., Men Are from Mars, Women Are from Venus

The course of true love never did run smooth.

William Shakespeare, A Midsummer Night's Dream

Thank you for your love, Father, that no matter where I am—in whatever situation—you are there loving me.

Billy Graham, Prayer for the Day, April 20, in *Day-by-Day with Billy Graham*

One of the realities after years of marriage is that whatever changes you had planned to make for that person are going to happen slowly or not happen at all.

Bill Cosby

Let us not love with words or tongue but with actions and in truth.

1 John 3:18

. . . And when you forgives you feels sorry for the one what hurt you, you returns love for hate, and good for evil. And that stretches your heart and makes you bigger inside with a bigger heart . . . you can lick the world with a loving heart!

Margaret Walker, Jubilee

It's incredibly easy to focus only on the negative aspects of your marriage or your mate. In doing so, however, you miss out on all the positive things. We make it a regular practice to count our blessings and talk about the other person's strengths and good qualities.

Couple, quoted in The Triumphant Marriage, *by Neil Clark Warren, Ph.D.*

The soul of a marriage can be a trysting place where two people can come together quietly from the struggles of the world and feel safe, accepted, and loved . . . or it can be a battleground where two egos are locked in a lifelong struggle for supremacy, a battle which is for the most part invisible to the rest of the world.

Keith Miller, The Taste of New Wine

I feel that God would sooner we did wrong in loving than never love for fear we should do wrong.

Father Andrew

It takes courage to face up to all the problems created by a complete adaptation of two personalities. . . . To come to understand that one's partner is very different—this already presupposes a great deal of personal growth.

Paul Tournier, To Understand Each Other

Let me assure you that romantic love and tenderness can be nurtured back to health even when the relationship seems beyond the grave.

Dr. James C. Dobson, Love Must Be Tough

Therefore encourage one another and build each other up.

1 Thessalonians 5:11

Whoever has loved knows all that life contains of sorrow and of joy.

George Sand

A successful marriage requires falling in love many times, always with the same person.

Mignon McLaughlin, The Second Neurotic's Notebook

Love has no awareness of merit or demerit; it has no scale by which its portion may be weighed or measured. It does not seek to balance giving and receiving. Love loves; this is its nature.

Howard Thurman, Meditations of the Heart

As God's chosen ones, holy and beloved, clothe yourselves with compassion, kindness, humility, meekness, and patience. Bear with one another and, if anyone has a complaint against another, forgive each other; just as the Lord has forgiven you, so you also must forgive. Above all, clothe yourselves with love, which binds everything together in perfect harmony.

Colossians 3:13-14, NRSV

Understanding Each Other

Have you noticed the words which Old Testament people use when someone important calls them by name? They don't say, "What?" or "Yes?" They answer with the curious sentence, "Here I am." So much is in that sentence: readiness to respond, a willing servitude, an offering of oneself to the other. But I rejoice in an even deeper meaning.

For there are times when my wife, Thanne, and I lie abed at night, nearing sleep. Almost we float apart from one another; sleep is so private an activity, and darkness seems to close us into ourselves. But then Thanne whispers, waking me: "Wally? Wally?" And suddenly the fact that she has called my name—that she knows my name and can say it, that she whispers it in the trust that I will hear her—makes me to know *me*. Her voice, her word, her presence startles me with the knowledge of selfhood. I distinctly realize, in the tingling darkness, that *I am*. Oh, that is a marvelous feeling—of being: an unspeakable gift of God.

Walter Wangerin, Jr., As for Me and My House

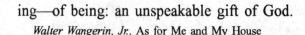

It's so difficult to know what the people we love really need.

Ugo Betti, Struggle till Dawn

Everyone today seems to be inwardly yearning for someone who really cares enough just to listen to him, without trying to change him.

Keith Miller, The Taste of New Wine

Though it cost all you have, get understanding.
Esteem her, and she will exalt you;
Embrace her, and she will honor you.
She will set a garland of grace on your head
and present you with a crown of splendor.

Proverbs 4:7-9

Love takes off the mask that we fear we cannot live with and know we cannot live without.

Robert Slater, The Pursuit of Loneliness

We are too quick to resent and feel what we suffer from others, but fail to consider how much others suffer from us.

Thomas à Kempis, Of the Imitation of Christ

True love contains an element of spiritual mystery. It embodies loyalty, reverence, and understanding.

Billy Graham, Day-by-Day with Billy Graham

Love is all we have, the only way that each can help the other.

Euripides, Orestes (408 B.C.)

Love is agreeing with him completely when he needs you to agree with him completely, and telling him the plain unvarnished truth when he needs you to tell him the plain unvarnished truth, and knowing when he needs which.

Judith Viorst, Love and Guilt and the Meaning of Life, etc.

Love enables us to do what love obligates us to do.

Lewis B. Smedes, Love Within Limits

There are no closed doors in love, no barriers, no limitations. If there were, God would not—could not love the world.

Eugenia Price, Make Love Your Aim

"Isn't it beautiful to think how everything has turned out . . . how they have come together again after all the years of separation and misunderstanding?"

"Yes, it's beautiful," said Gilbert, looking steadily down into Anne's uplifted face, "but wouldn't it have been more beautiful still, Anne, if there had been no separation or misunderstanding . . . if they had come hand in hand all the way through life, with no memories behind them but those which belonged to each other?"

Lucy Maud Montgomery, Anne of Avonlea

Love is not dumb. The heart speaks many ways.

Racine, Britannicus (1669)

When everything is verbalized about love and marriage there is still an intuitive element that remains as mystery.

The spirit of both husband and wife unite in greater depth than one can comprehend. This is why no one can fully understand on a purely rational basis the intricate balance of love in marriage. The mind cannot always grasp the deeper qualities of the spirit.

Elof G. Nelson, Your Life Together

I wanted to end this book with a wise and wonderful statement on how marriages work. I don't have a clue.

Erma Bombeck, A Marriage Made in Heaven . . . or Too Tired for an Affair

Deep sharing is overwhelming, and very rare. A thousand fears keep us in check.

Paul Tournier, To Understand Each Other

Don't be fooled by the face I wear. I wear a mask. I wear a thousand masks—masks that I am afraid to take off; and none of them are me.

Beneath lies no smugness, no complacence. Beneath dwells the real me in confusion, in fear, in aloneness. But I hide that. I panic at the thought of my weakness and fear

being exposed. That's why I frantically create a mask to hide behind—a nonchalant, sophisticated facade—to help me pretend, to shield me from the glance that knows. But such a glance is precisely my salvation, my only salvation, and I know it. That is, if it's followed by acceptance; if it's followed by love.

Dennis Waitley, Seeds of Greatness

No one of us lives, and equally no one of us dies, for himself alone.

Romans 14:7, NEB

"I'm a big-picture communicator, while Carol likes lots of details. I've been, and still am to some degree, a conflict avoider. Carol has been, and still is, more forthright. I grew up a 'pouter.' Carol's mom would not tolerate pouting. We've identified those items and have made major progress on all of them. And despite our differences, we are good communicators."

Minnesota husband, quoted in The Triumphant Marriage, *by Neil Clark Warren, Ph.D.*

One evening I was at a meeting and saw a young wife flash a grin and a wink at her husband, not because anything of consequence was happening, but because they were in separate groups and she wanted to establish contact with him. When he winked back I couldn't help but smile and think to myself that we get married as much for those winks as we do for anything else.

Eileen Silva Kindig, Goodbye, Prince Charming

None love, but they who wish to love.

Racine, Britannicus

One of the best ways to change me is to truly love me. Truly accept me. I think that's why people can say, after twenty years of marriage, "I know this woman has made me a better person."

William Willimon

"You my everythin, always. You my wife, my mama, my baby, my woman. My everythin."

J. California Cooper, Family

49

Grace finds pleasure in differences, encourages individuality, smiles on variety, and leaves plenty of room for disagreement. It releases others and lets them be.

Charles R. Swindoll, The Grace Awakening

She was thinking about the dream she had dreamed at Thanksgiving. It wasn't so much a dream as a feeling—a wash of intense, deep, perfect love. She had awakened and thought, For whom? and realized it was Ian. But it was Ian back in her childhood, when he had seemed the most magnificent person on earth. She hadn't noticed till then how pale and flawed her love had grown since. It had made her want to weep for him.

Anne Tyler, Saint Maybe

The "Phantom of the Perfect Couple" hangs over many marriages. They sleep spoon-fashion; we are separated by our dog who insists on licking herself at 3 A.M. They have pulled the plug on TV; our dinner conversations consist of yelling, "Buy a vowel!" at "Wheel of Fortune" contestants. They go out for regular date nights; we follow each other into the bathroom for a moment of adult conversation. They consult a financial planner on investments; we scrabble for loose change under the couch cushions. They entertain with gracious ease; we haven't had people in since the Reagan era.

The fact is, *they* aren't such flawless paragons and *we* aren't such hopeless bumblers. If we're honest, we'll admit we all meet at the middle somewhere, and God takes care of the rest.

Elizabeth Cody Newenhuyse

Preferring Each Other

Forgiveness, Faith and Hope

All of us forgive—on occasion, in a fragmentary way. And all of us have refused in certain situations. Because it was just too much to ask. We couldn't bring ourselves to do it, not immediately.

David W. Augsburger, Cherishable: Love and Marriage

You love me when I'm unlovable,
for didn't the Master say,
if you love those who love you,
so what?
Don't the heathen do that?

Unlovable.
I am that.
Perhaps we both are,
rather often.

But lovers speak their love
even when they hurt.
Thank you, Lover.

Harold Myra, Love Notes to Jeanette

But while he was still a long way off, his father saw him
and was filled with compassion for him; he ran to his son,
threw his arms around him and kissed him.

Luke 15:20, the return of the prodigal

Whom do you need to welcome back into your life right
now through your nonverbal expressions and words? Do
you need to express acceptance to your partner in some
way today? Each of us in our own way has played the part
of the prodigal. And when we turned toward home, God
smiled on us. Can we do any less toward those who need
acceptance, forgiveness, and affirmation?

H. Norman Wright, Quiet Times for Couples

Over the past several weeks I have seen God's severe
mercy at work. I am learning tough lessons in many areas

of my life, particularly in relation to forgiveness and rebuilding trust. I am profoundly grateful that in this process my husband and I are rediscovering one another in very satisfying ways.

Anonymous

When your heart aches with love, just the fear of having it thrust away is enough to frighten the boldest from spilling their simple truth.

Robyn Carr, The Troubadour's Romance

Everyone says forgiveness is a lovely idea, until they have something to forgive.

C. S. Lewis

Be kind to one another, tenderhearted, forgiving one another, as God in Christ forgave you.

Ephesians 4:32, RSV

I know that God will complete in me this work of mercy that he has started. He has already brought me—as the

African-American gospel song aptly puts it—a mighty long way in my outlook towards you. And, in the final analysis, how can I do less than pardon you for sinning against me, knowing that the Lord has forgiven all my wrongdoing.

Anonymous

He who forgives ends the quarrel.

African proverb

I love you! Even during terrible moments when I'm sure the overwhelming result of the death of either of us would be tremendous relief, I love you. I know this, because even as I'm licking my wounds and imagining all the delicious sympathy I would soak up at your funeral, my next thought is wondering if I put your clothes in the dryer . . . or wondering what you'd like for your birthday, or remembering a joke I wanted to share with you . . . and I'm impatient to make up so I can talk to my best friend again.

Elsa L. Braun Stewart, excerpt from a letter written to her husband on the occasion of their sixteenth wedding anniversary

We become persons of integrity by a lifetime of faithful decisions.

Chester A. Pennington, Liberated Love

Understanding is the reward of faith. Therefore seek not to understand that thou mayest believe, but believe that thou mayest understand.

Augustine

Where reason cannot wade there faith may swim.

Thomas Watson

Faith does not always correspond with reason; faith goes beyond reason. You must listen to the voice of God and his Word in the face of what others may say. No one said that faith is always easy. Sometimes you may struggle. But just consider the alternative—what would your life be like without any faith?

Adapted from Hearing God, by Peter Lord, in *Quiet Times for Couples,* by H. Norman Wright

For a moment, his eyes came back to her, wide and crystal gray, and there was admiration in them. Then, suddenly, they were remote again. . . . They were always like two people talking to each other in different languages. But she loved him so much that, when he withdrew as he had done now, it was like the warm sun going down and leaving her in chilly twilight dews. She wanted to catch him by the shoulders and hug him to her, make him realize that she was flesh and blood and not something he had read or dreamed. If she could only feel that sense of oneness with him for which she had yearned since that day, so long ago, when he had come home from Europe and stood on the steps of Tara and smiled up at her.

Margaret Mitchell, Gone With the Wind

It is necessary to hope, though hope should always be deluded; for hope itself is happiness, and its frustrations, however frequent, are yet less dreadful than its extinction.

Samuel Johnson, The Idler

The other night my husband Eric was sleeping and I was

propped up next to him, reading. I happened to glance over at him and noticed he was totally zonked, but was wearing what I always call his "Sister Martha Mary smile." It's a cute, mischievous, devil-may-care grin that I noticed the first night I met him and have always loved. Seeing it so unexpectedly, I smiled to myself and gently touched one corner of his mouth with my fingertip. By his reaction you'd think I had set off a bomb in the bed. He jumped three feet in the air, scrubbed vigorously at his face and mumbled, "What did ya do that for?" before flopping on his side so I couldn't do it again. What had begun as a tender moment ended in a sad, quiet loneliness. It reminded me that life's smallest incidents often probe our deepest hurts. And everybody has those hurts. *Everybody*.

Eileen Silva Kindig, Goodbye, Prince Charming

Love keeps us hopeful, in all situations, against all evidence.

Lewis B. Smedes, Love Within Limits

Whoso loves believes the impossible.

Elizabeth Barrett Browning

"I love you," he said without turning. "I want you to marry me."

"And you will love me forever and ever?"

"Yes. And you will worship the ground I walk on."

"And you will give me children before it's too late."

"And you will give me comfort and understanding."

"Yes."

And then, at last, he turned and held her tightly while they listened to the chapel clock strike seven and saw the bright light of afternoon soften to gray.

Camilla R. Bittle, Friends of the Family

And now these three remain: faith, hope, and love.

1 Corinthians 13:13

Love's Autumn

As a result of tending the garden during the summer, we get to harvest the results of our hard work. Fall has come. It is a golden time—rich and fulfilling. We experience a more mature love that accepts and understands our partner's imperfections as well as our own.

John Gray, Ph.D., Men Are from Mars, Women Are from Venus

To love is to make of one's heart a swinging door.

Howard Thurman, Disciplines of Spirit

There is nothing more lovely in life than the union of two people whose love for one another has grown through the years from the small acorn of passion to a great rooted tree. Surviving all vicissitudes, and rich with its manifold branches, every leaf holding its own significance.

Vita Sackville-West, No Signposts in the Sea

If twenty years were to be erased and I were to be presented with the same choice again under the same circumstances I would act precisely as I did then. . . . Perhaps I needed her more in those searing, lonely moments when I—I alone knew in my heart what my decision must be. I have needed her all these twenty years. I love her and need her now. I always will.

Edward, Duke of Windsor, on the occasion of the twentieth anniversary of his marriage to Wallis Warfield Simpson, for whom he abdicated the throne as Edward VIII of England

The horizon of marriage is new each morning, beckoning to further exploration of a dominion whose landscape is always changing, whose treasure is inexhaustible, whose promise is a call to unremitting hope.

Larry and Nordis Christenson, The Christian Couple

God is love and you both believe he is the author of your union. So the more you create channels through which his divine love can flow into your human love, the greater your love will be.

Charlie W. Shedd, Letters to Karen

We don't love qualities, we love persons; sometimes by reason of their defects as well as their qualities.

Jacques Maritain, Reflections on America

A really good marriage has the feel of a man and woman blending together into natural movement where individuality is obviously present but really isn't the point, something perhaps like dance partners of many years who anticipate each other's steps with practiced ease.

Dr. Larry Crabb, Men & Women

When, over the following months, Minta Randall found that Eustace apparently reciprocated her profoundest and most secret feelings, she thought she had never lived before, or knew what life could hold, or what absolute power one heart could exert upon another. She perceived no trace, fossil, or echo of this wild sensation anywhere around her, and concluded that she and Eustace had invented it together, which would be, she thought, just like them.

Annie Dillard, The Living

Two are better than one,
because they have a good
return for their work:
If one falls down,
his friend can help him up.
But pity the man who falls
and has no one to help him up!

Ecclesiastes 4:9-10

We have grown significantly through the years. I have become a cross-country skier, Jeff has become a family man, me a churchgoer, Jeff a helpful party-thrower, me a mountain woman, Jeff a flower-giver. I can't wait to see what God does with us in the coming years.

Wife, quoted in The Triumphant Marriage, *by Neil Clark Warren, Ph.D.*

Fun and Friendship

Hundreds of tense moments can be released with gentle humor which conveys to each person understanding, kindness, and the attitude "It really is amusing, isn't it?"

Elof G. Nelson, Your Life Together

She could be unexpectedly sweet and thoughtful, having his slippers toasting at the fire when he came home at night, fussing affectionately about his wet feet and interminable head colds, remembering that he always liked the gizzard of the chicken and three spoonfuls of sugar in his coffee. Yes, life was very sweet and cozy with Scarlett. . . .

Margaret Mitchell, Gone With the Wind

Let your fountain be blessed,
and rejoice in the wife of your youth,
a lovely deer, a graceful doe.

Proverbs 5:18-19, NRSV

The glory of friendship is not the outstretched hand, nor the kindly smile, nor the joy of companionship; it is the spirited inspiration that comes to one when he discovers that someone else believes in him and is willing to trust him.

Ralph Waldo Emerson

Friendship is even, if you like, angelic.

C. S. Lewis, The Four Loves

As the Father has loved me, so have I loved you. Now remain in my love. . . .
You are my friends if you do what I command.

John 15:9, 14

True friendship comes when silence between two people is comfortable.

David Tyson Gentry

We cannot tell the precise moment when friendship is formed. As in filling a vessel drop by drop, there is at last a drop which makes it run over; so in a series of kindnesses there is at last one which makes the heart run over.

Samuel Johnson

I've been married to you so long that we are switching roles. The other night, your laugh came out of me while I was watching TV.

Elsa L. Braun Stewart, excerpt from a letter written to her husband on the occasion of their sixteenth wedding anniversary

Later, when my husband came home, I said, "Guess what? I got a part-time job today."

"Doing what?" he asked.

"I'm going to write about funny things that happen to our family."

"You can't be serious," he said. "You're going to expose our personal lives to the public, exploit our children, and hold up our intimate moments together for the world to see?"

"I get three bucks a column," I said.

He smiled. "Why didn't you say so?"

Erma Bombeck, A Marriage Made in Heaven . . . or Too Tired for an Affair

When he comes home from work each day, he is likely to tell me about some paradox, something out of his usual routine, something that piqued his curiosity or annoyed him or, very often, something he thought was very funny. His wish is to amuse me. And we tease each other, sometimes flirtatiously. This kind of interaction has been a lively and important part of our daily life together for more than forty-five years. It is the dead opposite of taking someone for granted.

Judith S. Wallerstein and Sandra Blakeslee, The Good Marriage

Marital love experiences complex tensions that can create new phases of intimacy or can destroy the relationship. Married couples never need to take themselves so seriously that they cannot laugh at their mistakes.

Elof G. Nelson, Your Life Together

A sense of humor can help you overlook the unattractive, tolerate the unpleasant, cope with the unexpected, and smile through the unbearable.

Anonymous

Laughter is the closest thing to the grace of God.
Karl Barth

It's time we laughed!
After all, who should be laughing?
We, the forgiven!
We, the redeemed!
Who should be filled with joy?
We who have a million years,
to laugh and worship,
to leap for joy.
Harold Myra, Love Notes to Jeanette

If we love, we will not laugh at the wrong times. If we love, we will not withhold laughter when it is needed.
Eugenia Price, Make Love Your Aim

Let love be genuine; hate what is evil, hold fast to what is good; love one another with mutual affection; outdo one another in showing honor.
Romans 12:9-10, NRSV

71

An Enduring Relationship

Love's Winter

Then the weather changes again, and winter comes. During the cold, barren months of winter, all of nature pulls back within itself. It is a time of rest, reflection, and renewal. This is a time in relationships when we experience our own unresolved pain or our shadow self. It is when our lid comes off and our painful feelings emerge. It is a time of solitary growth when we need to look more to ourselves than to our partners for love and fulfillment. It is a time of healing. It is a time when men hibernate in their caves and women sink to the bottom of their wells.

John Gray, Ph.D., Men Are from Mars, Women Are from Venus

The memories of long love gather like drifting snow, poignant as the mandarin ducks who float side by side in sleep.

Lady Murasaki, The Tale of Genji (c. 1008)

Love will abide, eternally the same, when all the values we prize have died or been lifted into new stages of perfection.

Lewis B. Smedes, Love Within Limits

After she left, he went to bed and pondered what she had said. Could it be, he wondered, that love is stronger than death? Could it be possible that love is the strongest thing in the world? Water can't quench it, and death can't destroy it. How strange, he thought, that something so invisible and so fragile can be so strong.

Roberta Kells Dorr, Solomon's Song

Take away love, and our earth is a tomb.

Robert Browning

The thought of her brought him slowly to his feet. She would know what he had to do. She would clear up the rest of it, and she would at least be pleased. It seemed to him that, all along, that was what he wanted, to please her.

Flannery O'Connor, Everything That Rises Must Converge

Where there is love, there is pain.

Spanish proverb

I suspect that in every good marriage there are times when love seems to be over.

Madeleine L'Engle, Two-Part Invention

The world says (and your worldly flesh agrees) that it is your legitimate right, your dignity, and your duty to bring suit against the one who injured you, to press her until she has redressed the wrong, to accuse her, to punish her until her hurt at least is equal to yours.

[But] even before you face your spouse, it is absolutely necessary that you pause and self-consciously surrender the world and all its rights. You drop legalities. You die. Can you in fact do this on your own? Not often and never well. Only Jesus purely whispered from the cross, "Father, forgive them, for they know not what they do." It is Jesus who divorces you, not from your spouse but from the law, to place you fully under his light of grace. Here your faith, shaped by serious prayer, comes to life, for this is done in

trust alone; this is Christ's act and will therefore reveal Christ in your actions.

Walter Wangerin, Jr., As for Me and My House

Love cannot accept what it is. Everywhere on earth it cries out against kindness, compassion, intelligence, everything that leads to compromise. Love demands the impossible, the absolute, the sky on fire, inexhaustible springtime, life after death, and death itself transfigured into eternal life.

Albert Camus

When you are under pressure and feel like everything is collapsing around you, share your feelings with your partner. Pray about your trial specifically, expecting God to lift the burden and the fear. Take refuge in God, seek him, and receive his peace.

H. Norman Wright, Quiet Times for Couples

And there, on the edge of the field, was an old man, suitcase in hand. I knew in my heart that he had not been there two seconds before. He had appeared to me perfectly at once, as if he had been dropped standing upright from the clouds. I told my mother and grandmother to look at him. He was so still, staring at us. My grandmother looked up from the clothes basket, and without a word she started to run for him. At fifty-six, she ran like a young girl. He had given her nothing except sadness for so many years, but as I watched her fly into his arms, my thought was this: Oh, how she loves him. . . .

Kaye Gibbons, Charms for the Easy Life

Bitterness imprisons life; love releases it. Bitterness paralyzes life; love empowers it. Bitterness sours life; love sweetens it. Bitterness sickens life; love heals it. Bitterness blinds life; love anoints its eyes.

Harry Emerson Fosdick

You can see them alongside the shuffleboard courts in Florida or on the porches of the old folks' homes up north: an old man with snow-white hair, a little hard of hearing, reading the newspaper through a magnifying glass; an old woman in a shapeless dress, her knuckles gnarled by arthri-

tis, wearing sandals to ease her aching arches. They are holding hands, and in a little while they will totter off to take a nap, and then she will cook supper, and they will watch television, each knowing exactly what the other is thinking, until it is time for bed. They may even have a good soul-stirring argument, just to prove that they still really care. And through the night they will snore unabashedly, each resting content because the other is there. They are in love, they have always been in love, although sometimes they would have denied it. And because they have been in love, they have survived everything that life could throw at them, even their own failures.

Ernest Havemann, "Love and Marriage," *Life* magazine

That man has a "perfect" marriage. It may not be without its rough spots and trade-offs, but he feels absolutely wonderful about it. He is happy. Like a Japanese tea bowl, casually glazed and warped by the fire, his marriage, with all its idiosyncrasies, is perfectly beautiful, richly satisfying to behold in its irregularity.

Susan Page, Now That I'm Married, Why Isn't Everything Perfect?

When you love as she has loved, you grow old beautifully.

W. Somerset Maugham, The Circle

Love, though it expends itself in generosity and thoughtfulness, though it gives birth to visions and to great poetry, remains among the sharpest expressions of self-interest. Not until it has passed through a long servitude, through its own self-hatred, through mockery, through great doubts, can it take its place among the loyalties.

Thornton Wilder

They do not love that do not show their love.

William Shakespeare, Much Ado About Nothing

Happiness comes more from loving than being loved; and often when our affection seems wounded it is only our vanity bleeding. To love, and to be hurt often, and to love again—this is the brave and happy life.

J. E. Buckrose

81

Those who wait on the Lord shall renew their strength; they shall mount up with wings like eagles, they shall run and not be weary, they shall walk and not faint.

Isaiah 40:31, NKJV

A Wellspring of Renewal

After loving and healing ourselves through the dark winter of love, then spring inevitably returns. Once again we are blessed with the feelings of hope, love, and an abundance of possibilities. Based on the inner healing and soul searching of our wintry journey, we are then able to open our hearts and feel the springtime of love.

John Gray, Ph.D., Men Are from Mars, Women Are from Venus

They gave each other a smile with a future in it.

Ring Lardner

Love is swift, sincere, kindly affectioned, pleasant and delightsome; brave, patient, faithful, prudent, longsuffering, manly, and never seeking itself. . . .

Thomas à Kempis, Of the Imitation of Christ

Today, after twenty-six years of marriage, I am more sensitive to the thrill of her presence than I have ever been. When I come on her unexpectedly in a crowd, it is like a glad little song rising up somewhere inside me.

Charlie W. Shedd, Letters to Karen

Tomorrow [he thought] I'll sing for her the song I wrote after the first time I saw her. He hummed a few lines: "The winter is past, the rain is over and gone; the flowers appear on the earth." . . . With that he fell into a happy sleep and dreamed that he met a shepherdess dressed in thistle-gray. She looked just like Shulamit.

Roberta Kells Dorr, Solomon's Song

There is a rhythm in relationship, a rhythm that can only be heard as the great truths about God are played over and over again. Increasingly we recognize what they mean and embrace them as true: truths about his holiness and our sinfulness, about his yearning for relationship with us and the length to which he went to satisfy those yearnings; truths about how he has made us, and his good purposes for us;

truths about his indwelling, which means I live, yet not I, but Christ lives in me. . . .

   Dr. Larry Crabb, Men & Women

A great deal of time, in some cases years, is required for harmony to develop where each has learned how to respond to the other.

   Elof G. Nelson, Your Life Together

Commitment gives the marriage a chance. Commitment says, "Okay, I can't stand the guy today, but tomorrow we'll be laughing about it." Commitment gives the other *person* a chance—to grow and change and reveal the riches of his soul over time. My husband and I have been married eighteen years, and I feel like we're finally starting to get it right.

   Elizabeth Cody Newenhuyse

For yourself and for everyone around you, think right now about your spouse and the qualities you adore. Take the time to say something lovely that you have never said

before. Offer to do a favor. Think up a fun surprise. Enjoy each other, right now, for you will never have this moment again.

Susan Page, Now That I'm Married, Why Isn't Everything Perfect?

The long course of marriage is a long event of perpetual change, in which a man and woman mutually build up their souls and make themselves whole. It is like rivers flowing on, through new country, always unknown.

D. H. Lawrence, quoted in Creative Marriage, *by Mel Krantzler*

Love is patient, love is kind. It does not envy, it does not boast, it is not proud. It is not rude, it is not self-seeking, it is not easily angered, it keeps no record of wrongs. Love does not delight in evil but rejoices with the truth. It always protects, always trusts, always hopes, always perseveres.

Love never fails.

1 Corinthians 13:4-8

Words of and about Love

I love you no matter what you do, but do you have to do so much of it?

Jean Ilsley Clarke, Self-Esteem: A Family Affair

Love is blind.

Geoffrey Chaucer, The Canterbury Tales

Love is not really blind—the bandage is never so tight but that it can peep.

Elbert Hubbard

If kissing and being engaged were this inflammatory, marriage must burn clear to the bone. I wondered how flesh and blood could endure the ecstasy. How did married couples manage to look so calm and unexcited?

Jessamyn West, The Life I Really Lived

87

No one has ever loved anyone the way everyone wants to be loved.

Mignon McLaughlin

I looked at him as he returned the folding chairs to their original boxes. We had gone through three wars, two miscarriages, five houses, three children, nine cars, twenty-three funerals, seven camping trips, twelve jobs, nineteen banks and three credit unions. I had cut his hair, cleaned up his toenail clippings, and turned 33,488 pieces of underwear right side out. He had washed my feet when I was pregnant and couldn't see them, bought feminine products for me when I couldn't get out of the house, and put his car seat back to its original position after I had used it 18,675 times.

We had shared toothpaste, debts, closets and relatives. We had given one another honesty and trust. We had given our children something they weren't even aware of and took for granted . . . stability.

Erma Bombeck, A Marriage Made in Heaven . . . or Too Tired for an Affair

If we all discovered that we had only five minutes left to say all that we wanted to say, every telephone booth would be occupied by people calling other people to tell them that they loved them.

Christopher Morley

Love doesn't make the world go round. Love is what makes the ride worthwhile.

Franklin P. Jones

Captain Butler—be kind to him. He—loves you so.

Margaret Mitchell, Gone With the Wind

So let us . . . live as we ought;
Love is the lesson which the Lord us taught.

Edmund Spenser

Married couples who love each other tell each other a thousand things without talking.

Chinese proverb

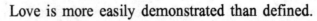

Love is more easily demonstrated than defined.

Anonymous

There is no more lovely, friendly, and charming relationship, communion, or company than a good marriage.

Martin Luther, Table Talk

The human soul is a lonely thing. It must have the assurance of companionship. Left entirely to itself, it cannot enjoy anything. . . . The only true cohesive power in the world is Christ. He alone can bind human hearts together in genuine love.

Billy Graham, Day-by-Day with Billy Graham

Love is or it ain't. Thin love ain't love at all.

Toni Morrison, Beloved

Your love, so solid and enduring, is like a mountain rising out of the plains. I can always look to it, receive comfort from its presence, and know it will always be there. Its beauty moves me. And it's a monument to how much I love you!

Gary Smalley and John Trent, Ph.D., The Language of Love

To love someone who doesn't love you is like shaking a tree to make the dewdrops fall.

Anonymous, Congo

Just as Miss Lavendar and Stephen Irving were pronounced man and wife a very beautiful and symbolic thing happened. The sun suddenly burst through . . . and poured a flood of radiance on the happy bride. Instantly the garden was alive with dancing shadows.

Lucy Maud Montgomery, Anne of Avonlea

I love you more than my own skin.

Frida Kahlo

Love is a little word; people make it big.

Anonymous

Love is the most durable power in the world. This creative force is the most potent instrument available . . . for peace and security.

Martin Luther King, Jr.

Daily, Hugh and I express what we feel, simply by saying and saying again, "I love you." Hugh and I have been saying it off and on for forty years. It comes off the lips of our children, our godchildren. It is all that needs to be said. I told Gretchen yesterday that Hugh and I have no unfinished business. There are no dangling strings left to be tied. I don't want him to leave me, but even more I don't want any more useless suffering for him. He is so gallant, so gallant, even today managing to smile for the nurses. For me.

I look at him, beautiful as an El Greco saint, for that is still the analogy that keeps coming to my mind. When I get home I look at a snapshot of the two of us together, Hugh's face alert and alive. I observe and contemplate this child of love, made of the same stuff as galaxies and stars. And I know that the only meaning is love.

Madeleine L'Engle, Two-Part Invention